D0241860

Aberdeenshire Library and Information Service
www.aberdeenshire.gov.uk/libraries
Renewals Hotline 01224 661511

3 1 AUG 2011

– 9 JUN 2014

2 3 DEC 2011

0 3 AUG 2012

– 7 MAR 2014
ABERDEENSHIRE
LIBRARIES

WITHDRAWN
FROM LIBRARY

BINGHAM, Jane

Eating
disorders

A L I S

2617900

Eating Disorders

Jane Bingham

WAYLAND

First published in 2008
by Wayland

Copyright © Wayland 2008

Wayland
338 Euston Road
London NW1 3BH

Wayland Australia
Level 17/207 Kent Street
Sydney, NSW 2000

All rights reserved
Series editor: Nicola Edwards
Consultant: Peter Evans
Designer: Alix Wood
Picture researcher: Kathy Lockley

The case studies in this book are based on real experiences but the names we have used are fictitious and do not relate to real people. Except where a caption of a photograph specifically names a person appearing in that photograph, all the people we have featured in the book are models.

The author and publisher would like to thank the following for allowing their pictures to be reproduced in this publication:
Mark Baigent/Alamy Images: 4, 15; Bubbles Photolibrary/Alamy Images: title page, 7, 22, 27, 43; Le Studio/AgenceImages/ Jupiter Images 12; CLEO Photo/Alamy Images: 20; Enigma/Alamy Images: 23; David J. Green/Alamy Images: Cover, 10; Sally & Richard Greenhill/Alamy Images: 21, 35; Charles Gullung/zefa/Corbis: 17; Angela Hampton/Alamy Images: 38; John Henley/Corbis: 19; Jack Hollingsworth/Corbis: 32; Crispin Hughes/Photofusion Picture Library: 39; Image100/Corbis: 13; Image Source/Corbis: 26; Ghislain & Marie David de Lossy/Image Bank/Getty Images: 16; Lisa Peardon/Taxi/Getty Images: 45; Jose Luis Pelaez, Inc/Corbis: 8; Photofusion Picture Library/Alamy Images: 9; Pixland/Corbis: 44; Ed Quinn/Corbis: 28; Rex Features: 33; Gary Roberts/Rex Features: 25; TWPhoto/Corbis: 37; Penny Tweedie/Alamy Images: 30: Wayland Archive: 14, 31, 36, 40, 42; Heiko Wolfraum/DPA/PA Photos: 18; Jerome Yeats/Alamy Images: 34; David Young-Wolff/Alamy Images: 41

British Library Cataloguing in Publication Data

Bingham, Jane
    Anorexia, bulimia and other eating disorders. - (Emotional
    health issues)
    1. Eating disorders in adolescence - Juvenile literature
    I. Title
    362.2'5

ISBN: 897 0 7502 4910 2

Printed in China

Wayland is a division of Hachette Children's Books,
an Hachette Livre UK company.

ABERDEENSHIRE LIBRARY AND	
INFORMATION SERVICES	
2617900	
HJ	661723
Y362.25	£12.99
YA	YAJ

Contents

Words that appear in **bold** can be found in the
glossary on page 46.

Introduction

Kim's favourite treat used to be going out for a pizza, but now she can't even bear the thought of it. Even though she's hungry all the time, she feels she can't allow herself to eat. When she looks in the mirror, she's convinced she's fat, and she hates the way her family and friends are always urging her to put on weight. Kim feels lonely, exhausted and scared. But she also feels that the only way to stay in control of her life is to be thin.

Anorexia and bulimia

Kim has **anorexia nervosa**, usually known as anorexia. People who have this condition – often known as anorexics – have an overwhelming need to be thin. They see themselves as overweight and so they deliberately **fast**, only allowing themselves to eat tiny amounts of food. Many anorexics also put themselves through a punishing programme of intensive exercise to prevent any weight gain. Anorexia is one of a range of eating disorders which also includes **bulimia**

A growing number of teens today experience some sort of problem with eating.

nervosa, known as bulimia. Bulimics (the term for people with this condition) alternate between frantic **bingeing**, when they eat huge amounts of food, and drastic **purging**, when they empty their bodies of everything they've eaten. Bulimics purge by making themselves vomit or by using **laxatives**. After a bingeing session, some bulimics also have a period of excessive fasting and exercise.

Unlike anorexics, who are painfully thin, bulimics are often of normal or above normal weight. But both groups have a very serious disorder. Anorexia and bulimia can affect people of all ages, but these disorders are most common among girls aged between 11 and 18. However, a growing number of teenage boys develop eating disorders too.

Find out more

This book gives you the facts about anorexia, bulimia and other disorders, such as **compulsive overeating**. It describes the physical effects of the disorders, and the dramatic impact they have on people's lives. It considers why so many teenagers develop difficulties with eating, and offers advice on how to seek help. Finally, it shows how people can recover from eating disorders and lead happy, healthy lives.

It's a fact: eating disorders

- It is thought that one in 100 teenagers has some kind of eating disorder.

- Around 10 per cent of teenagers with eating disorders are boys.

- About 90 per cent of people with eating disorders are aged between 12 and 25.

- More than half of teenage girls are, or think they should be, on diets. They want to lose all or some of the 18 kilograms (40 pounds) that females naturally gain between the ages of 8 and 14. About three per cent of these teens go too far, becoming anorexic or bulimic.

- About 1.2 million people in the United Kingdom experience eating disorders.

- About 8 million people in the USA experience eating disorders.

5

Chapter 1: *What is anorexia?*

How does anorexia start and how does it develop? This chapter shows what happens when a teenager becomes anorexic. It also explores the feelings and reactions of anorexics as their difficulties with eating take over their lives.

Deciding to diet

Anorexia usually starts with a decision to lose weight. There can be many reasons behind this choice (see Chapter 5). But, whatever the reasons, the basic decision is the same. A teenager feels unhappy with the way she or he is. So the teen decides to make some changes by losing weight.

In the early stages of anorexia, the teenager may decide to cut back on fattening foods, stop eating snacks between meals, or simply reduce portion sizes. All of this behaviour looks like an ordinary diet, which means that the first stages of anorexia can often go unnoticed. Friends and family may even praise the dieter for losing weight. But this cutting down on food can mark the start of a serious eating disorder.

Most teenagers don't diet for long. Without enough food to keep them going, they soon become hungry and tired and decide to give up the diet. But, in a few cases, this doesn't happen and the teenagers become at risk of developing anorexia.

It's a fact: anorexia

- In the UK it is thought that one in 100 females has anorexia, and one in 1,000 males.
- The highest rates of anorexia are found in girls aged between 13 and 19.
- Anorexia most commonly starts in the early to mid teens.
- Anorexia is one of the most common mental illnesses for young women.

It can be difficult for families to recognize the early stages of anorexia. Many parents believe that their teenager is simply on a short-term diet.

Taking control

Very few anorexics begin with the intention of losing lots of weight. But once they start to diet they feel a powerful need to continue. These teens discover that when they take control of what they eat, they feel much more in control of the rest of their lives. They have a sense of achievement as they watch the weight drop off. They also feel proud of their will-power as they manage to force themselves to overcome their feelings of hunger and weakness.

As they start to lose weight, some teenagers feel the need to test themselves more and more. At the same time, they become increasingly critical of their bodies and decide that they need to lose more weight. At this stage, their dieting usually becomes much more severe. They may start to skip meals, and drastically reduce the amount of food they eat. Anorexia has begun in earnest.

In focus: teenage dieting

There is a growing trend for teenagers to go on diets. In a recent survey, 40 per cent of American young teenagers reported that they dieted either 'very often' or 'sometimes'.

While the majority of teens who go on diets don't develop anorexia, they are still in danger of damaging their health. It can be harmful to cut down on food in the teenage years. This is a time when young people's bodies are growing fast and they need regular supplies of healthy food. Dieting can leave teenagers feeling weak and tired. See pages 8 to 11 to find out more about the dangers of teenage dieting.

Avoiding eating

Teenagers who develop anorexia soon learn strategies that allow them to eat as little as possible without people noticing. An anorexic teenager will try to avoid eating with friends and family whenever he or she can. The teen may cut up food into little pieces and eat very slowly. Some anorexics try to get rid of food secretly when nobody is looking. Sometimes anorexics make a show of eating normal amounts at a family meal, but severely restrict their intake for the rest of the day. All of these strategies for avoiding eating can disguise the problem until the eating disorder is well advanced.

Strategies to avoid eating also result in making the teenager increasingly isolated. When young people start to skip meals with their family and friends, they miss out on a valuable chance to socialize. Even when they are present at a meal, they cannot relax and enjoy the company, because they are constantly on their guard to stop others noticing how little they are eating.

Thinking of food

As anorexics try to avoid eating, they find themselves thinking more and more about food. Sometimes this **obsession** can take the form of counting **calories** – the units of energy contained in food. Many anorexics memorize exactly how many calories are contained in each type of food, so that they can work out how 'fattening' each food is. Some even weigh out the portions of food they

As anorexia develops, many teens avoid any situation where they have to eat with their friends. This means they miss out on a lot of fun.

Many anorexics take a great interest in food, preparing large meals for their family, but eating almost nothing of what they cook.

are planning to eat, so they can calculate precisely how many calories they will consume.

Even though they are eating very little food themselves, it is very common for anorexic teenagers to take a great interest in cooking. They may start to read recipe books, or they may cook elaborate meals for their family that they don't eat themselves. They may also urge their family and friends to eat more, while they are eating less and less themselves. All of these activities reflect the anorexics' unhealthy relationship with food.

In focus: *cutting calories*

Teenagers' bodies are developing and growing very fast, so they need to consume a large number of calories. The number of daily calories a teenage girl needs to be active and healthy has been estimated at 2,200, while active teenage boys need 2,800 calories. However, most anorexics consume fewer than 1,000 calories per day. When they cut down so drastically on the calories they consume, they are putting their health in very serious danger.

Feeling fat

Anorexics have a distorted **body image**. An anorexic boy may look in the mirror and see himself as fat even though he is really dangerously thin. An anorexic girl may become so scared of being overweight that she sees extra weight on her tummy, thighs or bottom, despite the fact that she is seriously underweight.

Too much exercise

Many people with anorexia push themselves to exercise, to burn off all the calories they have consumed. Teenagers who are developing anorexia will often start to walk faster than before. They may avoid sitting down and relaxing, and prefer to stand up or pace about.

As anorexia takes hold, teenagers may start to play more sport, or begin a regular exercise programme, such as doing lots of sit-ups, or swimming many lengths of the pool. It is common for anorexics to set themselves higher and higher

Teenagers with anorexia do not see their bodies as others do. When they look in the mirror, they see themselves as overweight. Even when they have lost a lot of weight, they remain critical of their bodies and push themselves to lose yet more weight.

10

goals, so they do a little more exercise every day.

This punishing programme of exercise can take up large amounts of time, making teenagers with anorexia even more cut off from their friends. Excessive exercise can also leave them feeling exhausted and weak.

Purging and pills

Some anorexics don't just restrict their food intake. They also purge their bodies of food by making themselves vomit or by taking laxatives. This kind of behaviour also occurs among people with bulimia (see page 18). It can be extremely damaging to the anorexic's health, especially when he or she is dangerously underweight.

Anorexics may also use other methods to keep their weight very low. They may smoke heavily or drink large amounts of alcohol to reduce their appetite. They may take diet pills to speed up the rate at which their body uses up its food. This has the effect of making them feel even weaker. They may also take **diuretic** pills. Diuretics make a person urinate frequently, so the body loses lots of water; this causes weight loss. However, taking diuretics can lead to dangerous **dehydration** (loss of water), which leaves the body without enough water to function properly.

In focus: family and friends

It can be very distressing for family and friends to watch someone they love experience anorexia. In this situation, many people feel tempted to urge the anorexic to eat, but this only has negative results. Within a very short time, mealtimes can become a battleground, as the anorexic becomes more determined not to eat, while family and friends grow increasingly angry and frustrated.

Mental health experts say that the most important thing that family and friends can do is to make sure that the anorexic teenager receives professional help (see Chapter 6). Meanwhile, they should try to keep mealtimes as stress-free as possible. Page 47 has a list of useful websites for the families and friends of people who are experiencing difficulties with eating.

Hungry and tired

People with anorexia wage a constant battle with feelings of hunger and exhaustion. Without enough food in their stomachs, they suffer from gnawing hunger pains. They also experience weakness and exhaustion because they are not eating enough food to provide their body with the energy it needs.

In this state of weakness, even the smallest physical effort becomes much harder. But despite their exhaustion, most anorexics still exercise excessively, making themselves even more tired. Many anorexics also find it very difficult to sleep, and this makes their feelings of tiredness even more extreme.

Feeling driven

Many anorexics are **perfectionists**. They are used to driving themselves to do their best, so when they decide to diet, they bring their usual

It's a fact: feeling the cold

As well as feeling hungry and tired, anorexics feel cold most of the time. There are two reasons for this:
- anorexics lack the usual covering of fat to keep them warm;
- anorexics suffer from poor **circulation**. As a result of fasting, the body does not receive enough energy to keep going as normal. So the heart reacts by slowing down and pumping blood around the body less vigorously than usual. This means that anorexics find it very hard to keep warm, and they usually have icy fingers and toes.

determination and will-power to the task of losing weight. Sadly, they soon become locked into the misery of anorexia.

As well as feeling driven to restrict their food intake and to exercise, many anorexics try very hard to keep up with their other activities as well. They still push themselves to excel at school, in spite of feeling weak and tired all the time. This effort is made especially hard because anorexia affects the ability to concentrate.

People with anorexia often have trouble sleeping. They may wake up frequently during the night, regardless of how tired they are feeling.

In focus: compulsive behaviour

Anorexia and other difficulties with eating may be forms of obsessive or compulsive behaviour. People who have **obsessive-compulsive disorder** (OCD) feel that their world is out of control, so they develop ways to try to control it.

Compulsive behaviour can take many forms. People with OCD may be obsessed by what they eat, or by being extremely clean or tidy, but they all establish certain 'rules' which they try to stick to rigidly. Following these rules makes people with OCD feel calmer and more in control, but breaking the rules can make them very frightened and panicky. OCD is a serious mental illness and can be treated by expert therapy.

Lack of concentration

One of the symptoms of anorexia is a loss of concentration. Apart from the distractions of feeling hungry, cold and miserable, anorexics find that their mental abilities are not as sharp as they used to be. Many teenage anorexics spend hours slaving over their homework, and still find their grades are slipping. Meanwhile, all their hours of hard work and study have the effect of making them even more cut off from their friends and family.

Depressed and isolated

As well as all the physical symptoms of anorexia, teens with the disorder experience many negative **psychological** effects. They become anxious, depressed, moody and irritable and often feel despair at their inability to cope with the demands of their lives.

Many teenagers with anorexia stop taking part in social events. They spend more and more time on their own, feeling isolated and cut off.

A teenager with an eating disorder can feel very lonely. He or she may feel that nobody understands what they are going through.

CASE STUDY

Kate was a quiet, hard-working girl who always did well at school. She had a small group of good friends. Then, when she was 13, things began to change. Her friends started ignoring her and hanging around with boys, and one day Kate heard them laughing at her.

Kate blamed herself for doing something wrong. She noticed that she'd put on some weight recently, and she didn't like the way she was changing. So she decided to go on a diet. In just a few weeks, she lost three kilograms (six pounds), and her Mum started nagging her to eat. Meanwhile, life at school was getting worse. She was even more cut off from her friends and now she was struggling with her work as well.

Kate made up her mind to diet even harder. At least, she thought to herself, this was something she could do really well. She also set herself a strict exercise schedule and got up early every morning to work out. As her weight continued to drop, Kate became more and more withdrawn. She stopped expecting anyone to understand her. Instead, she concentrated all her attention on her one really important goal – losing as much weight as she could.

Often, anorexics come into conflict with the people around them – especially when they are urged to eat. This makes them feel very lonely and misunderstood as they struggle alone with their disorder. Some teenage anorexics feel so isolated and despairing that they have thoughts of suicide, and a few even make the tragic decision to kill themselves.

As anorexia takes hold, it becomes much harder to concentrate, and work that used to seem easy takes much longer to do.

Chapter 2: *What is bulimia?*

The eating disorder of bulimia involves a pattern of behaviour known as bingeing and purging. First the bulimic eats a large amount of food and then she or he empties the stomach instead of digesting the food. This chapter describes the experience of teenagers with bulimia.

Cravings for food

People with bulimia experience cravings for food, which make them eat a large amount of food within a short time. The binge may involve eating large quantities of 'regular' food. However, it is much more common for bulimics to binge on the sorts of foods that they don't usually allow themselves to eat, such as cakes or biscuits or rich ice-cream.

There can be many underlying reasons why someone develops a craving for food, and these are explored in Chapter 5. However, bulimia often develops after a person has dieted rigorously and eliminated certain foods. After a period of feeling hungry all the time, people find themselves desperately craving food – especially the things they've forced themselves to give up. Once they give in to their urge to eat this food, they find they just can't stop.

Everyone has cravings for food they like, but people with bulimia can't control their cravings and find it hard to stop eating certain foods.

Feeling disgusted

Binges may last for up to two hours and often leave bulimics feeling so full that they simply cannot move. But once their craving has died down, they are left with a powerful feeling of shame and disgust. Not only are they furious with themselves for breaking the rules of their diet, they are also horrified at the thought of all the weight they will gain. Filled with disgust at their bingeing, bulimics decide to take drastic action to get rid of as much food as possible before it can be digested. So they purge themselves – by vomiting or by using laxatives.

It is possible to keep bulimia secret for a long time, so teenagers are often not aware that one of their friends is bulimic.

It's a fact: bulimia

- Bulimia is the most common eating disorder. The exact number of bulimics is unknown, though, because many people keep their condition secret.

- In the UK, up to four in every 100 women experience bulimia at some time in their lives.

- Bulimia commonly begins in the mid-teenage years.

- An estimated five per cent of all bulimics are male.

Many bulimics try to empty their stomach by vomiting. Apart from making the teenager feel dreadful, frequent vomiting has serious side-effects (To find out more about the medical effects of repeated vomiting see Chapter 4).

Purging

Bulimics can teach themselves how to vomit their food. Some learn how to make themselves sick by sticking their fingers down their throat or using an instrument, such as a spoon handle, to produce the **gag reflex**. This practice of deliberate vomiting can lead to a range of medical problems (see pages 24 and 27).

Many bulimics also use laxatives, in an attempt to expel as much food as possible from their bodies. Frequent use of laxatives can result in permanent damage to the kidneys and other internal organs. It can also cause heart problems and even heart failure.

A vicious cycle

Once bulimics have started to binge and purge, it is easy to start up a vicious cycle of disordered eating in which they indulge in regular overeating sessions and then try to empty the contents of their stomachs. In some extreme cases, bulimics completely lose control of their eating habits. They enter into a pattern of compulsive behaviour in which they overeat at every meal. This overeating is immediately followed by feelings of disgust and violent purging, and the cycle begins again.

Keeping secrets

Most bulimics feel intensely ashamed of their behaviour and so they do their best to keep it hidden, bingeing on their own and making secret visits to the bathroom. This secretive behaviour can have a bad effect on their relationships. It is common for an atmosphere of distrust to build up, as family and friends begin to suspect what is going on.

In this situation of distrust and suspicion, a bulimic teenager can become increasingly withdrawn. Many bulimics feel that they have to struggle with their problem alone. They can feel scared and isolated as they try to cope on their own with strong feelings of shame and guilt.

CASE STUDY

After six weeks on a very strict diet, Jo was miserable. She was constantly hungry and thinking of food. Then, one day, something snapped. She found herself raiding the kitchen, and eating a whole tub of ice-cream, swiftly followed by six doughnuts and a packet of biscuits. It felt like something had taken over her body, and she simply couldn't stop stuffing herself.

When she finally finished, Jo felt sickened and deeply ashamed. How could she have broken her diet and lost all her self-control? She decided the only thing to do was to get rid off the hated food, so she went to the bathroom and locked the door…

Jo soon became expert at getting rid of food. In just a few weeks, she was bingeing and purging every day. She had entered the secret and destructive cycle of bulimia.

When teenagers try to hide the fact that they are bulimic, things can get very tense at home. Parents can become suspicious and even angry, and teens can feel resentful and alone.

Chapter 3: *Bingeing and overeating*

Anorexia and bulimia are not the only problems people have with eating. Many teenagers feel compelled to eat too much. Just like anorexics and bulimics, they have an unhealthy relationship with food, and are putting their health at risk.

Binge-eating disorder

People with binge-eating disorder frequently eat huge amounts of food at a single session. Just like bulimics, they have powerful cravings for certain foods and when they binge they feel that they have lost control. After bingeing, binge eaters experience powerful feelings of disgust, shame and remorse. However, unlike bulimics, they do not purge after they have binged.

Most teens with binge-eating disorder are overweight, but some are normal weight. Often they try to keep their condition secret and struggle to cope with their eating problems on their own.

Many overweight teens suffer from teasing. This can make them even more likely to turn to food for comfort.

People who binge and overeat may choose foods that are high in fat and sugar, which adds to their feelings of guilt.

Compulsive eating disorder

People with compulsive eating disorder eat large amounts of food even when they are full. This abnormal eating behaviour may happen all the time, or it may come and go in cycles. Compulsive eating disorder usually develops as a way of coping with stress, as people use food to comfort themselves. They may see eating as a way to escape from their troubles, but the habit can rapidly spiral out of control.

Teenagers who overeat on a regular basis can easily get locked into a vicious circle. They feel depressed because they are overweight, so they eat compulsively to make themselves feel better. However, this behaviour makes them more depressed, which leads to more compulsive eating.

Compulsive overeaters put their health at risk by being overweight (see page 23). They also suffer from depression and very low **self-esteem**. As well as struggling with overeating, they have to cope with others' lack of sympathy for their situation.

CASE STUDY

When Dan was nine years old, his Dad left home and his Mum became very depressed. Dan and his Mum spent a lot of time at home, watching TV and eating, and by the age of 12 he was already overweight.

At school, everyone called Dan names and he was always left out of the football team. To make himself feel better, Dan turned to food. Even when he wasn't hungry at all he found he needed the comforting taste and feel of food in his mouth.

In the end, things got so bad that Dan was eating almost constantly. He no longer recognized whether he was hungry or not, he just knew that he desperately wanted to eat. He hated the way he looked and felt, but he didn't know how to stop his powerful cravings for food.

Chapter 4: *Symptoms and effects*

What are the signs that a person is developing an eating disorder? Sometimes a dramatic change in weight alerts others to the problem, although weight loss or gain is not always present in bulimics. However, other signs may become evident. People with eating disorders often change their behaviour. They also have some physical **symptoms**, which provide a clue to their disordered eating patterns.

Changing behaviour

One of the first warning signs that a teenager may be developing an eating disorder is a change in behaviour, as the person becomes more secretive and withdrawn. If someone is developing bulimia, he or she will start making visits to the bathroom after meals. Teenagers in the early stages of anorexia begin skipping meals and make excuses to eat very little. Often they will avoid certain foods (especially fattening ones), and they may announce a dramatic change in food preferences, such as a switch to a vegetarian diet.

When teenagers start to refuse food they used to enjoy, they may well be developing anorexia.

Other signs to watch out for – especially if you suspect that someone is becoming anorexic – are irritability and moodiness, sleeplessness, and a deliberate avoidance of social occasions. Teenagers who are developing anorexia often become hyperactive, indulging in frequent vigorous exercise and rarely sitting still.

Anorexia – the physical signs

As anorexia develops, several physical symptoms appear. The most obvious of these is dramatic weight loss. Other physical signs are thinning hair, brittle nails and dry, flaky skin. These symptoms are a direct result of the body receiving too few **nutrients** to replace its skin, nail and hair cells efficiently.

Anorexics often have red or purplish hands and feet caused by poor circulation. They usually grow fine, downy hair on their face, arms, stomach and back. This fine hair, known as **lanugo**, is a means of preserving heat as the anorexic's body temperature drops.

In focus: bingeing and overeating – signs and effects

Compulsive overeaters are overweight, and teenagers who binge usually have a weight problem too. These groups of teenagers can suffer from a wide range of health problems caused by carrying too much weight. They may experience back pain and problems with their joints. Their excessive eating can damage their digestive systems and their internal organs, especially their liver and kidneys, while carrying too much weight puts excessive strain on their heart and lungs.

Many overeaters have very high blood-sugar levels, which can easily develop into **diabetes**. Even if they do not experience health problems in their teens, they are building up many problems for later in life.

Carrying too much weight puts your body under a lot of strain. Sooner or later, seriously overweight people will develop problems with their health.

Bulimia – the physical signs

Many bulimics have a puffy-looking face with swollen cheeks, giving them a chipmunk-like appearance. These physical changes are caused by the expansion of the **salivary glands** in the cheeks. Whenever someone vomits, the salivary glands produce large amounts of saliva. In bulimics who vomit regularly, these glands become enlarged, causing swollen 'chipmunk' cheeks.

People who have bulimia often develop swollen stomachs, ankles and fingers, because of a lack of **protein** in the body. This deficiency is a side effect of the regular use of laxatives, which strips the body of many valuable nutrients.

Many bulimics also have crumbling or discoloured teeth. When they vomit, their mouth is filled with acid from the stomach, and frequent contact with the powerful acid wears away the enamel that protects teeth.

Medical effects

Some serious physical changes underlie the signs and symptoms of eating disorders. Many of the effects of an eating disorder can be reversed once the teenager starts to eat normally again, but some damage is permanent. That is why it is very important to try to seek medical help as soon as possible.

Circulation problems

Most anorexics have very low blood pressure and poor circulation. In response to the reduced amount of energy delivered through food, the anorexic's heart pumps more slowly than normal. This change causes blood pressure to drop, as the blood takes longer to travel around the body.

Low blood pressure results in dizziness, faintness and headaches. Poor circulation means that the anorexic is always cold. People with anorexia often suffer from chilblains – rough, red, itchy patches of skin caused by a reaction to cold.

In focus: putting off puberty

Girls and boys who develop anorexia before they have entered puberty do not experience the changes to the body that are associated with growing up. For example, girls do not develop breasts and boys do not grow body hair. But when they start to eat normally once more, they go through the usual changes of puberty.

No more periods

As anorexic girls start to lose significant amounts of weight, they stop having periods. This is another of the body's automatic responses. Regular periods are a sign that a woman's body is ready to bear children, but without enough energy delivered through food, the ability to have children automatically shuts down.

Usually, regular periods return once a girl starts eating normally again, although this can take some time. After a girl has returned to her normal weight, it may be up to a year before her periods return. In a few cases, a recovered anorexic may not have any more periods, or she may have problems getting pregnant. However, such effects usually only happen to long-term anorexics.

Some anorexics become so weak that they barely have enough strength to walk – let alone have children.

In focus: *severe depression*

One of the most dangerous effects of eating disorders is depression. Depression is caused partly by the feelings of loneliness and isolation that come with an eating disorder, but it has physical causes too. Anorexics and bulimics lack many of the hormones, minerals and vitamins that help to maintain an even mood.

When teenagers with eating disorders deprive themselves of vital nutrients, they affect the balance of chemicals in their brains, making their depression more severe.

Brittle bones and teeth

Anorexics and bulimics lack calcium, as well as other important nutrients in their diet. Calcium is essential for building bones, especially during the teenage years. Teenagers who develop eating disorders before they have finished growing, may fail to achieve proper growth.

Long-term anorexics and bulimics are at risk of developing **osteopenia** (brittle bones). This condition can result in broken bones and in the curving of the spine in later life.

Lack of calcium in the diet also affects the teeth, making them weak and subject to decay. This problem is most severe for bulimics, whose teeth are also attacked by the acid in their vomit. Some bulimics have to have all their teeth capped.

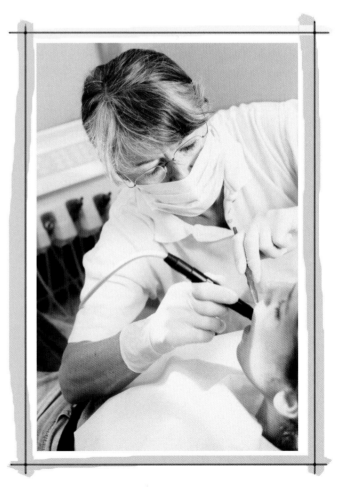

Teenagers with eating disorders usually have to spend a lot of time at the dentist.

26

When teenagers abuse their digestive systems, they can experience some painful symptoms.

causes irritation to the stomach and the **digestive tract**, so the bulimic suffers from painful burning sensations in the chest and stomach. Some bulimics lose control of their gagging reflex, so vomiting happens automatically every time they eat.

Stomach problems

Anorexics and bulimics also suffer from intense stomach pain. As anorexics reduce their intake of food, their stomach shrinks dramatically, so eating even small amounts can cause severe discomfort and **bloating**. Many anorexics also have digestive problems. Some experience diarrhoea, while others have painful constipation.

Bulimics can develop similar digestive problems when they abuse laxatives. Frequent laxative users have painful stomach cramps. They also suffer from **chronic** diarrhoea or constipation.

The practice of forced vomiting also results in problems. Frequent vomiting

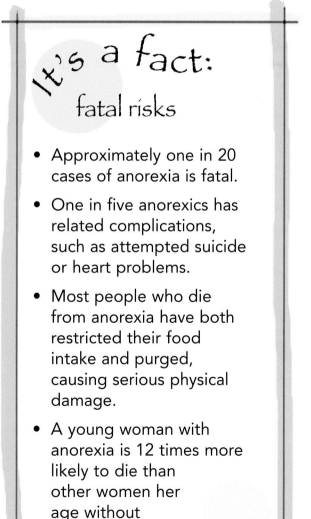

It's a fact:
fatal risks

- Approximately one in 20 cases of anorexia is fatal.

- One in five anorexics has related complications, such as attempted suicide or heart problems.

- Most people who die from anorexia have both restricted their food intake and purged, causing serious physical damage.

- A young woman with anorexia is 12 times more likely to die than other women her age without anorexia.

In focus: *heart problems*

People with anorexia put their hearts under a massive strain because they eat too little. This strain is increased if they also exercise too much. Meanwhile, the heart is deprived of essential tissue-building minerals, such as potassium, and its muscles start to waste away. People who use laxatives put their hearts in particular danger, as laxatives strip the body of almost all its potassium.

Many anorexics and bulimics experience heart **palpitations** and dizzy spells. People with long-term eating disorders often develop heart problems, and, in extreme cases, they can die from heart failure.

Wasting muscles

As anorexia becomes advanced, muscles weaken and waste, especially in the upper arms and the legs. This damage is caused partly by a lack of potassium and other minerals. Also, once the body has used up all its reserves of fat for energy, it starts to consume muscle tissue instead.

Damaged organs

Anorexia and bulimia can have harmful effects on all

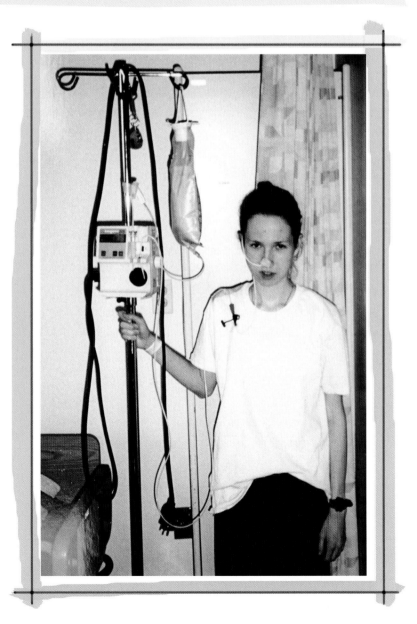

Some anorexics have to be admitted to hospital and put on a drip to provide their bodies with the essential minerals they need.

body organs. People with these diseases lack essential minerals, such as potassium and sodium, and this causes their organs to be seriously weakened. Imbalances in blood sugar levels can stop the liver from functioning properly. The repeated use of laxatives and diuretics causes dehydration which can result in serious damage to the kidneys. Meanwhile, the nervous system ceases to function properly and the brain is also affected. Complex thinking and concentration become increasingly difficult, as too little oxygen reaches the brain.

A fatal combination

Around one in 20 anorexics dies from the condition. For a small percentage of these people, the cause of death is a heart attack or liver failure. However, the vast majority of deaths are caused by a combination of factors. As their disease progresses, anorexics become progressively weaker and develop more physical problems. At the same time, they become increasingly depressed. They finally reach a stage when they can no longer take part in normal life, and suicide can seem to be the only option.

CASE STUDY

Lucy first developed anorexia when she was 12. For the next six years, she survived mainly on a diet of tomatoes, rice cakes and water. Just occasionally, she would allow herself to eat larger amounts, but after these episodes she always purged drastically, forcing herself to vomit and using laxatives and diuretics. Despite being incredibly weak, she exercised for up to three hours a day.

At the age of 18, Lucy looked like a desperately ill ten-year-old. Her arms and legs were stick thin, with wasted muscles, but her joints and stomach were swollen. She had the early signs of liver failure, and she suffered from constant dizziness and heart palpitations. She had been in and out of clinics many times, but she always left as soon as she could and started on her punishing routine once again.

By her 18th birthday, Lucy was so weak she was forced to spend most of her time resting. But she still kept starving herself and pushing herself to exercise. A week after her birthday she collapsed with a massive heart attack. Just as her old school friends were starting out on their adult lives, Lucy was dead.

Chapter 5: *What causes eating disorders?*

What causes teenagers to become anorexic or to develop bulimia? And what makes some young people overeat? Sometimes it can be hard to find the exact answers to these questions. Every teenager who struggles with food has their own, individual reasons for developing their disorder. However, many young people face similar pressures which help to contribute to eating disorders.

Under pressure

Eating disorders generally develop as a response to pressure or stress. Everyone has to deal with some kind of pressure, but stresses can be especially intense at certain times in your life. As young people approach puberty and the teenage years, many

As children become teenagers, they start to look at themselves in a new way. A few feel unhappy with what they see and decide to make changes.

Reacting to pressure

Faced with all these stresses, it's not surprising that some teens feel their lives are out of control. Some of them turn to food as an area where they can take control, and make their own decisions about what they eat. Other teenagers may see food as a form of escape, and may start to binge or overeat.

of them experience a lot of pressure.

Girls and boys in their early teens have to deal with increasing stresses at school. At around this stage, schoolwork becomes much more demanding than before and there are also exams to face. Teenagers may come into conflict with their parents or other adults as they try out their new independence. They may also feel under pressure from their friends – to keep up with the latest fashions and to look good for the opposite sex.

◄ *Some teens feel under pressure from all sides – their parents, their school teachers and even their friends. These stresses can lead them to develop an eating disorder.*

In focus: *teens at risk*

Two groups of teens are especially likely to develop eating disorders. Teenagers who already have serious problems in their lives are especially vulnerable (see pages 36-37). But other teens at risk are high achievers – boys and girls who appear on the surface to be successful, attractive and confident but who have always pushed themselves in order to succeed.

Some high achievers set very high standards for everything they do and they blame themselves whenever they fail. As teenagers, they face new challenges which can make them feel anxious and self-critical. Some teens respond to these pressures by turning to dieting as a way of 'testing' and 'improving' themselves.

Diet danger

One of the major stresses faced by teenagers is the pressure to be thin. Everywhere they look – in magazines and newspapers and on TV – they see criticism of people who are overweight. They also see advertisements for diets that are supposed to change people's lives. The message given out by the media is loud and clear: if you want to be happy, popular and successful, you need to be slim.

Once girls start to develop curves, they grow even more aware of all the media pressure to be thin. At this stage, many girls become very critical of their own shape or size. Some of them decide that life would be much better if only they were very slim, and so they start to diet. A growing number of teenage boys also feel pressured to have a lean and muscular body, and so they make the decision to take control of what they eat.

Peer pressure

It isn't just the media that drives people into dieting. Teenagers also experience lots of pressure from their peers. If they are even slightly overweight, they may have to face teasing and cruel remarks. But sometimes the pressure isn't as direct as this. Girls may hear their friends talking about diets or simply notice that some girls are slimmer than they are. These experiences can push teens to begin dieting.

Super-thin celebrities

Often the media concentrate on women and girls who are extremely skinny. Today's magazines are full of

Magazines often use altered photographs of women that make the women look thinner than they actually are. Images like these can give the reader a false idea of the kind of body shape that can be achieved by dieting.

photographs of super-thin celebrities. Many fashion models are also extremely thin, with almost childlike bodies. A few models may be naturally willowy, but most of them admit that they have to diet very hard to stay so thin. There have been several cases of models with anorexia or bulimia.

Even though there are articles in the media pointing to the dangers of being very underweight, teenage girls are still confronted by many images of super-skinny models, actresses and celebrities. These women usually dress in expensive clothes and look very glamorous, so it's not surprising that many teenage girls dream of being as thin as them.

In focus: the super-skinny debate

Recently, some groups have campaigned to ban ultra-thin models from fashion shows and magazines. In response, a few designers have agreed not to employ models who are unhealthily thin. However, some members of the fashion industry have resisted such a ban.

Images of super-skinny models can sometimes make a normal, healthy teenager feel self-conscious about her size. It's hard for teenagers to keep reminding themselves that they are fine just the way they are, when they are surrounded by images of models who are extremely thin.

Sporting pressures

Teenagers who want to excel at sports need to be super fit. They have to put in many hours of training to keep their bodies at a peak of fitness, and sometimes they even need to keep to a certain weight. Dancers and gymnasts are expected to stay extremely slim, while wrestlers and boxers have to control their weight in order to stay within various categories such as 'flyweight' or 'middleweight'.

Some young people respond to the pressures of their sport by depriving themselves of certain foods, or putting themselves on a very strict diet. At the same time, they may increase the hours they spend in training. These can be the first steps on the path to a serious eating disorder.

Boys get eating disorders, too

A growing number of teenage boys are experiencing eating disorders. Some are compulsive overeaters or bingers, but boys also develop anorexia and bulimia. Today, one in ten people with an

Teenagers who are training as dancers or gymnasts are under great pressure to stay slim. Most of them eat healthily, but a few respond to this pressure by cutting down on food.

eating disorder is male. Teenage boys may develop anorexia after they have been teased about their weight. Or they may simply decide that they want their bodies to look lean and toned.

Boys have less body fat than girls, which means that their condition usually goes unnoticed for longer. So, by the time the eating disorder is recognized, the individual is often in urgent need of help.

Boys can feel under just as much pressure as girls to change the way they look.

CASE STUDY

George was a shy, slightly chubby boy, who had always felt awkward about his body. He never took his top off, even on the hottest days, and he hated swimming because he felt that everyone was laughing at him. Then one day he made a decision. He would put himself through a training programme until he had a hard, toned body like the athletes he admired.

George soon discovered that trying to gain the perfect body was very hard work. He got up early to go for runs and worked out with weights whenever he could, but he still felt that he was too fat. So he decided to cut down on food as well. Once George started dieting, he soon noticed the difference – and his family did too. They began to worry that he was going too far. They also found that he had become moody, withdrawn and irritable.

Even though George had dramatically changed his body shape, his life at school didn't get any better. In fact, he noticed that people were looking at him even more strangely. But he was determined not to give up everything he'd achieved. Instead he pushed himself even harder, eating less and exercising more. When he collapsed from exhaustion, other people finally recognized the severity of his illness.

Escape from the adult world?

There are many reasons why teenagers develop anorexia, but some anorexics describe their wish to stop their bodies maturing. Having a childlike body can seem very appealing to some teenagers, who see it as a way to escape from the choices and responsibilities of the adult world. So a teenage girl may choose to make herself look like a child as a way to avoid the pressures of dating, and the unwanted attention of boys.

Sexual abuse

In a few cases, teenagers retreat into anorexia or other eating disorders after an experience of **sexual abuse**.

These **traumatic** experiences can make the victims feel frightened of their sexuality or disgusted by their own bodies. As they struggle with their negative feelings about sex, some teens react by developing an eating disorder. Some may start overeating as a way of giving themselves comfort. Others may develop a destructive pattern of bingeing and purging, as a response to their sense of disgust at their body, or they may decide to retreat into the safety of childhood, and develop anorexia.

Extra pressures

Some young people run a high risk of developing eating disorders because of the major problems they have to

Some troubled teenagers feel very unhappy about joining the adult world. For them, it seems safer to stay as a child. By losing lots of weight, they make their bodies child-like, and so avoid the possible problems of the world of adults. However, they create a whole new set of problems for themselves.

face. These troubled teens may come from homes where there is constant conflict or even violence, or where a parent is struggling with addiction or illness.

Other teens may suffer from depression or be involved in drug-taking, drinking or crime. Teenagers faced with problems like these can feel that their lives are dangerously out of control. In these circumstances, it's not surprising that some of them develop eating disorders as a way of regaining control over some part of their lives.

A family problem?

There is evidence that a tendency to eating disorders can be passed down from one generation to another. In particular, the problem of compulsive overeating often runs in families.

Teenagers also learn their eating habits from their parents. For example, a child with a parent who is very concerned with dieting is much more likely to go on a diet than a child brought up in a family where everyone eats healthily.

In focus: eating disorders – West and East

Until recently, anorexia and bulimia were much more common in western Europe and the USA than in the East. However, that situation is changing. Over the last ten years, Japan, Korea and China have all experienced a dramatic rise in the numbers of people with these eating disorders.

In Japan, the percentage of anorexics increased tenfold between 1980 and 2000. Some experts say the increase is partly the result of the influence of Western cinema, TV and magazines.

As society in Japan becomes more Westernized, the number of Japanese people with eating disorders is rising sharply.

Chapter 6: *Getting help*

It is possible to make a complete recovery from an eating disorder. However, it can be hard for teenagers to recover all on their own. Fortunately, there are plenty of people and organizations to help.

Recognizing the problem

The first and most significant step on the road to recovery is to recognize the problem. Denial, both on the part of young people themselves and their families, is the main reason why eating disorders progress so far without being treated. Once a teenager admits that she or he has difficulties with eating, the first vital move has been made in breaking away from negative patterns of thinking and eating.

At this stage, it's vital to seek outside help. Teenagers may decide to talk to a parent, a school counsellor, or a friend, who can help to put them in touch with some expert help. Some teens choose to talk to someone who does not know them personally. They may ring a helpline or visit an internet site. There are many organizations that offer advice on different treatments and experts to contact. Page 47 has a list of websites and helplines.

Talking over problems can be a great relief – especially with an experienced therapist. Many teenagers feel that they are finally able to discuss all the things that have been really worrying them.

Getting help

The first stop for medical advice is often a teenager's family doctor. Some doctors undertake the treatment of eating problems themselves, but many refer their patients to a **therapist**, a psychiatrist or a specialized clinic.

Therapists in eating disorders look at the reasons underlying their patients' problems with food. They also help people with eating disorders to develop healthy eating patterns and change their perceptions about body image and food.

It's a fact:

long-term outcomes

- Approximately half of all anorexics and bulimics make a full recovery.

- About 30 per cent make a partial recovery.

- About 20 per cent experience no major improvement.

- On average, anorexia lasts for 1.7 years.

- On average, bulimia lasts for 8.3 years.

As well as having regular therapy sessions, teenagers with eating disorders may also be given advice on diet and nutrition. **Nutritionists** discuss with their patients how much they should eat in order to stay healthy, and explain what kind of foods they need in order to get all their essential minerals and vitamins.

Sometimes people with eating disorders need medical attention for the physical problems the disorder has caused. Once they resume healthy eating patterns, many of the physical effects are reversed.

Nutritionists give advice on how to achieve and maintain a healthy body weight.

Therapy

Therapy for eating disorders involves regular sessions with a therapist, in which the patients discuss their thoughts and feelings. These sessions help the young people to understand more about why their disorder started. The therapists also help them to change the things in their lives that made them turn to food to gain control.

One of the most important elements in recovery is the development of greater self-esteem, so therapists work hard at helping their patients to value themselves more. Once a teenager has a better sense of self-worth and wants

Regular therapy can be an enormous help in building up a teenager's self-esteem and problem-solving abilities.

to be healthy, it is much easier to return to normal eating patterns.

Different approaches

Most therapy takes place in one-to-one sessions, but sometimes a small group of people with a similar problem is treated together. Group therapy can be very valuable, as participants compare their thoughts and feelings, and support one another in their efforts to get well.

Sometimes, family members are included in sessions, with the young person's permission. Parents may also be seen in a separate session. In these sessions, the therapist helps the parents to understand why their child developed an eating disorder, and also suggests ways in which they can help their teenager to recover.

One step at a time

Recovery from an eating disorder can take weeks, months or even years and, during this period, there can be many setbacks. Therapists encourage their patients to take small steps towards normal eating, and not to expect too much from themselves straight away.

It is common for recovering teenagers to have some days when they seem to slip back into old patterns. Good therapists urge their patients not to feel disheartened and remind them of the progress they have made.

In focus: keeping a diary

Many therapists encourage their patients to keep a diary. This journal should be an honest record of everything they eat and it should include notes about the writer's changing moods and thoughts.

Writing a diary can help recovering teenagers face up to their eating habits. Once they see their food intake written down, they can realize just how little (or how much) they are eating. The diary also helps them to recognize the link between their feelings and thoughts and what they are eating. As teenagers work at returning to normal eating patterns, their journal helps chart their progress.

Keeping a diary is a good way of working out exactly how you feel.

Case Study

When Anna was admitted to hospital with anorexia, she weighed less than 27 kilos (60 pounds) and she was dangerously weak and dehydrated. She was given an intravenous drip for the first 48 hours. Then she was fed through a tube into her stomach until her weight reached a safer level. Once she was strong enough, Anna was encouraged to start eating again, beginning with very small amounts of food. Expert nurses monitored everything she ate and gave her lots of support and encouragement. Anna made good progress and, within a few weeks, she was able to leave the hospital ward and attend a residential treatment programme.

At the clinic, Anna had regular sessions with a therapist. She also joined a group of anorexics, who discussed their problems with food and gave each other support. Anna felt for the first time that she was able to talk freely about her condition. She also felt relieved to be away from all the rows with her family. At the same time, Anna's parents received counselling sessions, and stopped putting pressure on Anna to eat.

In the supportive atmosphere of the clinic, Anna made a very good recovery. There were still days when she felt tempted to return to her dieting, but most of the time she just felt lucky to be well and strong again.

Serious cases

Some teenagers with eating disorders put themselves in serious danger. They may have heart problems, or damaged organs, such as kidneys or livers. In cases like these, patients have to be admitted to hospital where they can be given emergency treatment for their medical problems.

Anorexics who have become dangerously thin and weak may need to be fed intravenously

Some teens struggle for years with their eating problems. They need support and understanding to help them overcome their problems and return to healthy eating patterns.

(through a vein) or through a tube directly into the stomach. Once they have gained enough strength to feed themselves, they receive small amounts of food at frequent, regular intervals. Because the anorexics' stomachs have shrunk dramatically, food has to be introduced very gradually, as they slowly build up to normal-sized meals.

A tragic end

Sadly, not everyone with an eating disorder makes a full recovery. Some people struggle with eating disorders throughout their adult lives. They become increasingly weak and usually die early from a range of causes – either from organ failure, or from a heart attack, or by suicide.

Some teens who have been extremely ill manage to make a full recovery. They may benefit from regular meetings with support groups.

Chapter 7: *Staying well*

A large proportion of teenagers with eating disorders make a full recovery. After a period of struggling with food, they manage to establish healthy eating patterns. So what can teenagers do to help themselves stay well, and how can they make sure that they don't develop destructive eating patterns?

Healthy eating

Whether someone feels tempted to eat too much or too little, the best way to beat those feelings is to establish a pattern of regular, healthy meals. Skipping meals is never a good idea, as it can easily lead to over eating at the next meal.

It is best to try to avoid foods, such as cakes and biscuits, which make you feel full up quickly but soon leave you feeling hungry again. Instead, go for meals that provide you with a slow release of energy that will keep you going until the next meal. Slow energy release foods are high in **fibre** so they take longer to digest. They include fruit and vegetables, muesli, and wholegrain

Eating a diet that is rich in fresh fruit and vegetables gives you energy and, along with taking regular exercise, keeps your body in good condition.

bread. Brown rice and wholegrain pasta are also high in fibre.

Keep off the diets

Unless someone is **clinically overweight** and has been given medical advice to diet, it's best to stay well away from diets. Putting the body on a strict diet disturbs its natural rhythms. Strict dieting can trigger anorexia, or lead to a pattern of bingeing and purging typical of bulimia.

People come in all sorts of shapes and sizes. Recently, there has been a strong reaction against unnaturally thin models. Now most people recognize that women and girls who are the proper weight for their height look strong, healthy and attractive.

In focus: taking action!

If you think that you are developing unusual eating patterns – or if you're worried about one of your friends – take action now. Talk to someone you know and trust about your concerns. Or turn to page 47 for a list of organizations and people to contact.

Energy for life

During the teenage years you need plenty of energy – and that energy comes from eating regular, healthy meals, from taking moderate exercise and from getting plenty of sleep. If you have a healthy lifestyle, you will end up feeling and looking good. Then you can get on with enjoying your life, instead of worrying about weight and food.

Eating shouldn't have to be a cause for worry. Sharing food together can be one of life's pleasures.

Glossary

anorexia nervosa An eating disorder, in which people feel an overwhelming need to be thin. People with anorexia see themselves as overweight and only allow themselves to eat tiny amounts of food. Anorexia is short for anorexia nervosa.

bingeing Eating very large amounts of food within a short period of time.

bloating Swelling of the stomach, caused by trapped air inside the intestines.

body image The mental picture that a person has of his or her own body.

bulimia nervosa An eating disorder, in which people binge on large amounts of food, and then try to empty their bodies of the food by vomiting or taking laxatives. Bulimia is short for bulimia nervosa.

calories Units used for measuring the amount of energy contained in any food. The number of calories in a food also indicates how 'fattening' that food is.

chronic Long-term and serious.

circulation The movement of blood around the body.

clinically overweight So overweight that the person's health is in serious danger.

compulsive overeating An eating disorder, in which people feel an overwhelming need to keep on eating even when they are full.

dehydration The loss of water from the body.

diabetes An illness that causes people to have too much sugar in their blood.

digestive tract The part of the stomach where food is digested and absorbed through the stomach walls into the blood.

diuretic Causing people to urinate frequently.

fast To go without food for long periods of time.

fibre The part of some foods, such as cereals, fruit and vegetables, that passes through the body but is not digested.

gag reflex The natural instinct to bring up food, caused by something being put down the throat.

lanugo Fine, downy hair that grows on the face and body of anorexics, as a way of helping to keep them warm.

laxatives Substances that cause people to go to the toilet.

nutrients The parts of food that nourish the body.

nutritionist An expert on healthy eating and the effects of food on the body.

obsession A state of constant preoccupation with something.

obsessive-compulsive disorder A psychological disorder, which causes people to become very anxious about things in their life. People with obsessive-compulsive disorder (also known as OCD) often develop patterns of behaviour from which they cannot escape.

osteopenia Low bone density.

palpitations Rapid heart beats.

perfectionist Someone who aims to be as perfect as possible in everything that she or he does.

protein A substance found in some foods, such as eggs, milk, cheese, meat and fish, that helps bodies to grow and repair themselves.

psychological To do with the mind and the emotions.

purging Getting rid of food from the body, by vomiting or taking laxatives.

salivary glands Small organs in the cheeks that produce saliva, to keep the mouth moist.

self-esteem The sense of being happy with the way you are.

sexual abuse Having a sexual or a physical relationship with someone against their will.

symptoms Signs of an illness or a problem.

therapist Someone who is specially trained to give help, support and advice to others.

traumatic Very upsetting and shocking.

Further information

Books to read

Grace Bowman, *Thin* (Penguin, 2007)

Deborah Hautzig, *Second Star to the Right* (Walker, 2001)

Jo Kingsley, Alice Kingsley, *Alice in the Looking Glass: A Mother and Daughter's Experience of Anorexia* (Piatkus, 2005)

Beatrice Sparks, *Kim: Empty Inside: The Diary of an Anonymous Teenager* (Arvon, 2002)

Organizations to contact

BEAT

A UK-based charity, dedicated to beating eating disorders.
Website address: **www.edauk.com/**
Telephone helpline: 0845 634 7650

A telephone 'youthline', especially for young people with concerns about eating disorders. Youthline is open Monday to Friday 4:30pm-8:30pm; Saturdays 1:00pm-4:30pm

To request a BEAT counsellor to call you back, text callback and your name to 07786 20 18 20

Helpful websites

www.familydoctor.org/online/famdocen/ home/children/teens/eating/277.html
Information for teens from doctors, including Q&As and a list of resources.

www.doctorann.org/weight/
Advice for teens from a doctor, including responses to teenagers' letters.

www.kidshealth.org/teen/your_mind/ mental_health/eat_disorder.html
Part of the Kids' health website, aimed at young people and teenagers, presenting clear information on eating disorders. There is advice for friends on how to help someone who is having difficulties with eating.

www.anred.com/
Clear and detailed information on anorexia, bulimia, binge eating and other eating disorders, with advice for parents on how to help a child who has eating problems.

www.youngminds.org.uk/
The website of a national charity that aims to improve young people's mental health. It includes information on and sources of help for eating problems.

www.healthyplace.com/
Information on many aspects of mental health, including eating disorders, with a section aimed at parents.

www.edap.org/
The website of the United States' National Eating Disorders Association aims to promote the understanding of eating disorders and to encourage people affected by them to seek treatment. It includes sections aimed at the parents and friends of people with eating disorders and gives advice on how they can help.

Index

Page numbers in **bold** indicate pictures.